"The Shapes We Make"

by Dan Smith

thedancemyth.com

2025

I want to thank my sweet love and partner Kath for supporting me in so many ways through the making of this project. I would not have given it a real shot if it weren't for her pointing me back to myself when I kept questioning if this was worth putting in the work for. I know now (and I'm sure I'll forget and have to relearn it again) that no matter what, it's worth it… even and especially if it's just for me.

"The Shapes We Make" is a talk music album (under the artist name "dance myth") and now/instantly a book of meditations and poems to pause and sit with. If you want you can follow along with the album or just be here now, like you already are.

I'm glad you are here.
You got you here!
Thank you for taking the time
with and for yourself.

"This isn't for you, it's for me."

Now repeat that sentence
until you are ready to move on,
and then move.

Gentle, Gentle

We
   are
      not
         just
            the
               sum
                  of
                     who
                        we've
                           been.

All of us.

         Complicated angels.

                        Strange,
                  and beautiful,
            and weird-of-a-kind.

The world is magic.
How else can it be?

Be gentle.
Gentle!

When the pain gate opens wide.
Swallows us in whole.
Building the things we are gonna need,
but we can't see it yet.

Some
kinds
of
lightning
don't
want
to
be
seen.

We
 get
  jump-started
   into
    this
     thing
      with
       a
        purple
         rain
          storm,

           and
            end
             up
              with
               a
                grey
                 heart

                    full of rocks.

Busy,   on our way to right now.
Speeding,   towards this second.
Showing up, early for the next one.
Pushing us, to our next meaning.
Different,   every time we try.

Gentle now.

We are not
just the sum
of our mistakes.

We   live   so   many   lives,

in   a   day,

and   we   numb   most   of   it   away.

Forgive   yourself.

If   you   can.

For   who   you   you've   been.

You   didn't   know   then.

I have spent most of my life running.
As hard as I can.

Breaking things,
and then try to fix them.

Behind my back.
So you can't see the mess I'm making.

Here, can you fix it?

be careful. Careful!

This
is
all
I
get.

I'm gonna make mistakes,
and then mend,
and then do it
over and over again.

Maybe forever.

Try to show my work
while I'm working it out.

How else do I do this?

We are not just simple math.

We are a library of surprises
inside a maze of last stands.

We are magic.

We are Magic!

The
echoes
of
our
foremothers.

Writing trains.
Following where they lead.
Stretching words over a life,
written in water.
It's as simple as a circle.
I was raised by holding on
and living in it.

And
 it
  might
   not
    get
     any
      easier
       than
        this,

              but Love.

         It's
          worth
           all
            you're
             fighting
             for.

              Especially
               if
                it's
                 for
                  yourself.

Complicated angels.
You are everything.
A soaring revelation
inside of your circle.
Returned back into you.

The Light

Can we agree
to not fully understand,
and let that be?

We can feel how temporary
this whole this is, yeah?

The wet paper frailty of being human.
Inside our hand me down perspectives.
Fragile and thread bare.

Loose leaning
against each other's
loose meanings.

Full of holes,
and worn through.

We
only
get
away
with
this
for
so
long.

Trading our time
for some coins
to throw in a well.

But I am still water,
and this is still life,
and I am still mine.

I am a bomb rattling in my chest.
A hammer, crashing through.
A mountain of failures.

I am, the whole sun.
A sputtering star.
A hung breath disappearing.

I am an exclamation!
An idea machine.
All the colors combined.
Outlined.
With both Hands open.
Writing love notes to myself.
About the lights in my life.
From sun-bright, to pink cotton.
Around, again, for another try,
and
then
take
off
in
every
direction.

Glowing
      through
            all
               the
                  shapes
                     I
                        make.
Through
      the
         copper
             holes
                in
                  my
                     heart.

A punctuation of light.

Aflame,
electric,
in every direction.

Look at what your light did now.

I keep writing love notes
to myself to:

Write about joy!
And the ways I follow it.

And how much I've grown to know that

Love

is the first letter
in acceptance,
and change,
and you!

It's there if you're looking for it.
I promise it.
It's inside of you.
Already.

You Daredevils,
& dreamers.
Rolling under a turquoise mountain,
crackling into the night.

Another.
World.
Is possible.

If you want it.
If you make it.

You Pioneers,
    pushing your miracle
        around the pavement.

        Sparking
        and scraping.

        Escaping
        into your shapes.

        Spinning
        and Wide eyed.

The inventor of your worlds.
    A body
    underlined
    a thousand-thousand times.

Strapped to the front of the ride.

I can see "it" all over you.
Marked by all the births
you've been through,
to get you here.

You grew some more today.

I keep writing these love notes
to myself to:

Say about the fire
that was put into me

to heal,

when I didn't know how to.

Got talked into dimming down.
Forgot how to fly.
Didn't think I could.
Cut my hair boring.
Couldn't sing every word.

But my Friends-in-Love.
Pulled me up from my free fall.

Helped me burn every bridge
        to light the way
                to what's next.

You
   reminder
    mountains!

Pushed
   me
     back
       onto
         my
           volcano,

        and we rang out.

We
  rang
   out
    like
     iron
      bells
       hung
        in
         the
          arms
           of
            oak
             trees,
                and
                carved
                the
                words:
                    "keep going".

     And so I keep exploding
     out
     in every direction.
     Like the sun.
     Young and love.

Saying songs about
what became of that boy.

Wandering out loud.
Trying everything,
and then give it all away
so there's nothing left to lose.

Staggered
blocks.

Little
probletunities.

On the edge of an impossibly wild ride
that I won't survive.

I have been alive before,
and I'll be alive again.

And I have been dead too,
and I will die over and over again.

Spread out In every direction.

Like the sun.

So,
If you are alive.
Raise your hands.
Keep them open.
Reach out for anyone.

Little Bird

It all started in a hospital bed.
    when they made up the words
        to say you were gone.
            Said you didn't make it,
              to where we were.
    As if where we were was better.

So
 I
  fell
   down
    backwards
     inside
      my
       bottom
        lip.
Collapsed
  into
   a
    dead
     weight
     black
     out.
Spun
  myself
   into
    a
     thread,

and backed out of all my stitches.

I woke up inside the tv.
Toes
    on the edge in the brake dust.
Left shoulder
        baked in a lightning bath.
Head
    dull and grainy.
        When
        all
        the
        air
        pulled
        out
        and
        stopped.

I was a little wet bird,
walking around a forest fire.

Seat belted
right next to a bruised miracle.

Sat behind a woman
  broken
into a thousand ways to say:

Never. Give. Up.

So she didn't.

You had a sea glass halo.
Pinned to a cloud with wishes kisses.
Surrounded by your loves.
Waving goodbye.
Singing something about leaving,
but
  it
    wasn't
      in
        a
          language
            that
              we
                worry
                  over.

We   built   a   world
and   colored   it.

Cut out cardboard castles to candle light.

Made   up   songs
to   sing   joy
through   our   greys,
and   our   whites.
Smiling   inside   of   October.

And   when   that   second   Christmas   came
we   held   each   other's   gifts.
The   sky   wept,
and   we   haven't   been   the   same   since.

I wasn't ready
        to do the dance
                that everyone else
                        seemed suited for,
in my magic light blue suit.
Quarters coming out of my ears.
Both hands filled with shape of your absence.

Sorry,
you
couldn't
make
it,

to
where
we
were.

As
if
where
we
were
was
better.

You were gone,
to everywhere else.
Back into the air we breathe.
Back into everyone I meet.

Carrying the zero.
Sharing your math.
Smiling at all the joys
that came to you.

And most days
        I can't stop
            waking in circles.

                A head full of brake dust.

                Alive at the wheel,
                through the morning rays.

                Shining
                 through
                 all
                   the
                    shapes we make.

So I sit on that road.

One arm in a sling.

Where the wind

goes over the wing,

and open up my mind

as big as it will go.

As big as this floating globe.

Push my soul through my teeth,

and stitch my way back to home.

I wake up inside the tv,
and see a little wet bird
asleep in a hospital bed.

One wing longer than the other,
and a life
opened up as big as it will go.

What an unending place.

Waking Up To Your Island

You are a failure miracle.
Brand new, again.
A rising sun.

Exactly, everything you need,
and enough.

Writing out your morning song.

You are the answer,

     inside of a long exhale.

A lighthouse rib cage.

     A future up for grabs,

     and the brights are on.

There is a point inside of you.
a light,
a start,
a shy,
quick,
quiet,
deer heart.

A lighting storm.

One Machine for rain,
and the other for change.
Buried in your covers,
in color.
A new day tapping at your eyelids.
My shy,
quick,
quiet,
deer hearts.

You are a failure-miracle.
Tangled in truth.
Folded around with love.
Plugged back into yourself.
Waking up to your island.

You,
are a
self governed machine.

A harpoon,
launching.

A bell,
rung against the collective order.

An entire world,
rising.

Brand new,
again.

You failure-miracle.
Still and silent.
Stretched to your horizons.
Up at dawn.
Waving your existence.
A pride swallowing siege.
A hug,
instead of a hammer.
A spark,
inside of a room.
On top of all this dirt.
Dressed
in
your
first
day
of
school
innocence.
Shy,
quick,
quiet.
Suited in universe.

The divine.
Tied to the present.
Making it through the night.
A metaphor for infinity.
A waking celebration,
bathed in light.
Waking up to your island.

You failure-miracles.
Brand new, again.

Remembering,
and forgetting,
and remembering.

Quilted together.
Burning the past for change.

Into this moment,
and this one,
and the next one,
and the next one,
and this one right here.

The most important moment
of your life   are all the ones
you are   inside of.

Brand new, again.

Make It Until You Make It

I   keep   telling   myself,
that   I   keep   telling   myself,
that   I   keep   trying.

        But I've been forgetting again.

Forgetting   that   it's   happening.
This   presence   of   awareness.
A   closeup   of   clarity.

                    What a wake!

I shouldn't have to remind myself. Again.
That this is not a rehearsal.
There is no script.
Our lives mix poorly inside each other
sweating badly to fit.

Making it until I can make it.

I have never done this before.
How are you so sure?

We are given once our hearts,
and our bodies, are sinking ships.
Bailing out the bad parts.

Looking for the laugh.
Bracing for the launch.
Hanging in there,
   waiting for the universe to show up.
Breath held for an answer.
Life pushed to the side.
Right hand
   lit up like a Christmas tree.
Pointing at the truth,
in our hearts,
where it's always been.

Making it
while I figure this out.

Still.

I'm still figuring this out.
How are you so sure?

Time,
  is
    how
      we
        count
          the
            things
              we
                waste.
But that's easier said than done.

Life
  has
    this
      way
        of
          coming
            around.
Hope mixed with waiting it out.

    It doesn't make sense now,
  but long games are sure things
      that let us figure it out.

          Figure it out!

Even if it's just inside of me.
There's no better place put the plow.
Inside all the caves I make.
On the other side of my moonbeam.

Squinting,
　forehead first.
　　At the bottom of the world.
　　Where all the oceans meet.
　　Anchor in the air,
　　　outlined in sun.
　　　Making it
　　　　until I can
　　　　make it on my own.

And I keep trying
　and trying.
　　How are you doing this?

And just to be sure.
I have never done this before.

Like right now
I can feel my heart
pulling at the reigns
wanting to change.

Like it's done hundreds
of thousands of times
before today.

And sometimes I follow it.
And sometimes I weigh it down
with whatever I find laying around
that will keep me from the pain of change,
from the change of pain.
Am I doing this again?
It's gonna take a lifetime to get it out.

Get it out!

Like when I was young,
    and there wasn't this
        weight of perspective,
            and time moved slower
                than the growing pains.
Going to sleep when it was still light out,
    with tears in my eyes.
      There was always so much more to see.
Making it.
    While I try to Make it.

I
have
never
done
today
before,
but
I'm
willing
to
try
it
again.
Clawing
at
the
bark.
Trying
to
feel
something.
Making it
until
I
make it.

This Accordion life

You don't know me.
No one really does.

That's just the shape of smoke
    from setting myself on fire.
        Lit from the inside.

Floating above.

If
you
want
problems
get
a
future
and
survive
it.
No
one
really
does.

Tomorrow is terrifying.
The past is terrifying.
But in the right now,
right now,
right now.
Right now I am aflame.

Inside of a life coming apart.
At home in a minor key.
This accordion life,
with you.

I was holding back the porch
on a Halloween weekend.
Sun-set in my eyes.
We Had a fire on.
Played a new tune on the keys.
Kept thinking about jumping,
or spreading out.
Always leaving something behind.

Even the kindness of absence.
Or a clear head.
Or my cannonball heart.
Stuck inside a crack in the sky.
Inside a forced answer.
Rolling my Rrrrrs.
Packing the anxiety furnace.
Racing in slow motion.

I
will
always
be.
A presence carved in wake.
A better version of yesterday.
Four thousand weeks away.

I found the words I wrote
in the back of the van,
pushed into the seat.
The one we kept for sleep
when we were out for months on the sea.
Melting and folding myself back into me.

I told myself:

> that getting better
> means I have to keep going,
>
> and so I did.

Inside of a life
coming apart.
Right at home
in a minor key.
This accordion life,
      with you.

I'm better alive.

      Waking to your absence.
      While the weeks go by the window.
      Outside that hospital garden.
          Inside a dead end.
      Working at forgetting about it.

It's embarrassing.

All the times I've hidden,
or was made to feel I should hide
any of the ways I shine.

Told everyone I'm fine,
and believed that lie myself.

Into one more fall,
   and then another,
      and another one.

Until I'm falling again.
   And giving everything,
      every time,
         everywhere.

Stretched to the edges of me.
   Surrendered to the exhale.
      Sanding down the shimmer.

Leaving what makes this scary,
   and stunning.
      A mirror
         to what I'm becoming.

You don't know me.
        No one really does.
That's just the shape of smoke.
        From setting myself on fire.
Lit from the inside,

        floating above.

Inside
  this
   life
     coming
      apart.
At
  home
   in
     a
       minor
        key.

Out of all the things
that I'll miss the most
inside this accordion life.
An entire heart away.
I'll miss the fall,

                     with you.

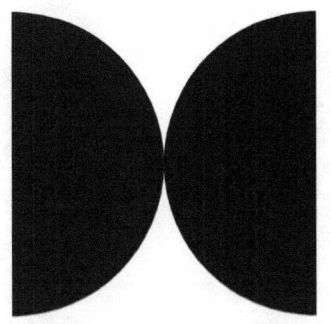

Playing Pretend

We
all
woke
up
one
day.
A light,
turned on.
Into our existence.
Into sound and cold
and confusion.
Just like everyone else
who has ever done this.
Even the ones of us
who have touched the sky.

Shoved right into a costume
that will never fit.
And every day is halloween,
clashing against
our intuition.

We
all
woke
up
one
day.
Every.
Single.
One of us.
Looking out of our miracle.
Bolted to reality.
A metaphor for a mystery.
Loved by the wonders that made us.
In their own ways,
that they learned how.
That got hammered into them,
by wolves,
just trying to make it.
Playing pretend.

We   all   wake   up   one   day.
Blanketed   in   fear.
Collared   with   reality.
Get   given a   dog   in   the   fight
by   the   wolves   that   raised   us.

They said:
Our imaginary friend,
it's better
than everyone else's imaginary friend.

Dug those walls right into us
against our better sense.

Tied our balloon to a closed down mind,
and family and worth.

We all wake up one day.
With everything we need
already inside of us.
And still take someone else's word for it.

Willing to hold that as truth.
Instead of listening to our own.
And point that thing into our inevitable.

Writing the answers on our sails
so we don't forget again.

    We are all playing pretend.

We   will   all   wake   up   one   day.

Just   like   everybody   else   does.

Just   like   god   did.

You   can   see   her   everywhere,

in   every   thing.

I
  don't
   use
    words
     when
      I
       pray,
        that's
         a
          waste
           of
            the
             answer.
              I
               keep
                my
                 hands
                  and
                   everything,
                  open.

That's where the answer is,
in the open.

In the wild, dull sparkle.

The space between
          heaven and hell
          is the distance
          between faith and doubt,
          in ourselves.

We will all wake up one day.
        Into our existence.
Powerful miracles
        wrapped in skin.
Pushed down by drink,
        and age,
        and the learning
        that we can't.
Shamed smooth by our mistakes.
Forgetting our accents,
        and the roads we learned on.

But we are who we pretend to be.
So don't just do something.
Sit there, and think it through.

You could die at any time.
But then again
you could live at any time too.

Glass Maze

Right outside of here
is where we smash against each other.

Skin on skin.
Skinny straw blades against the storm.

Bending the hard way.

Mistakes on high.

Young and old,
graceless.

We have no chance,
            and it's only in our minds
that we have no choice.

There is always choice,
we always have it.
            Welcome to life.

Entire
libraries
built
inside
of
people
have
been
lost.
      Keep making.

Bend your life
into anyone
you can see.

Forehead against forehead.

Spilling everything
inside our frail machines.
Full of stupidity.
Distracted with Energy.

Weighing us down
with enough hope
that we might
have a chance
to stay longer.

There will always be change
to teach us balance
To show us common sense.

If we're willing.

Person against person.
Bringing us back to learning.
Where shame lifts like a curtain,
and it's our time to dance.
Have you had enough flailing?

Take time to be kind,
and also to yourself.

Build the future,
  together.
   With your hands,
    with your loves.
     Pounding time
      into its permanence.
       Folding it on top of itself.

Our skin
made out of sandpaper,
wearing each other down
until we're shorter,
worn down with memories,
and the choices we've decided on,
or passed over,
or lucked in to.

What a mess.
What a thing.
What a life.

We are all playing pretend.
Crashing into each other.
Waking up with brand new hearts
that only work
when we make them die
over and over again.
Inside this glass maze.

It's the only way,
and that's just for today.

Dry County

I was in the dead center
  when the sky turned green,
   and a pile of shoeboxes
    shook their contents loose.
    Into blue envy.
     Onto wet power lines.
     Lonely strangers
      in a gravel ditch,
       right over there
        where the firewood
         used to be stacked.

I held Up my neck like a wheat stalk.
Blood orange and burnt red.
Waving inside an Arkansas sunset.
Waving like I had to go.

But I was out there
stuck in the rain.
Talking about the weather,
and I couldn't see the sky,
except by ambulance light.
Flickering
against
the
smoke.

Like A bird
on its way.

On a scarecrow.
Protecting what's in sight.

It's all lost.
It's all for nothing.
It's gonna to be alright.

And I was waving.
Waving!
Waving like i had to go.
I was right there
waving like i had to go.
Waving, like i had to go.
And so I went.

I left half a cigarette next to a spider web.
I   had   other   things   to   do,
and   never   looked   back.
That's   as   useless   as   coffin   paint.

Inside another all nighter.
A full head, and sandy.
Fingers interlocked
in the legs of that thing.
While the leaves crawl out
from their branches.

Racing
  our
    trains
      down
        the
          highways.
            Next to the trains
              we sleep to at night.
                Racing through our thoughts
                  in the pitch black.
                    Lit up by headlights
                      and hope.

Under the sheets
washed at half strength.
Inside that motel
with the chainsaw angel.
Holding a sword
above a sign
that's never said "no".
There is always room
for those who fight.

It's all a blur.
It's all a lie.
It's gonna be alright.

And she was waving!
    Waving like she had to go.
        She was right there waving
            like she had to go
                Waving,
                like she had to go.
                And so She left.

We held hands.
    Leaned ourselves into the future.
        Joined the parade from the train bridge,
            and swam the lake.
                Made promises to our shadows.
What a kindness.

Putting
our
pieces
together

while the leaves stretch out on their
                                branches.

Smoothing
our
edges,
learning
where
our
county
lines
lie.

A blanket
        of mistakes.

With good Intentions,
        and bad memories,
            and a god dam in our
                            hearts.

A ghost,
inside of a man,
inside of a room.
Watching the leaves fall
for their own reasons,
without a fight.

Cuz it's all over.
It's all a mess.
It's gonna be alright.

You were waving
 like you had to go.
  You were right there waving
   like you had to go.
    Waving, like you had to go.
You had to.

And it may be comforting,
or scary,
or both,
or none of it.

But one night
in the hands of death.
There will be a sign
with your name on it
tied to nine balloons,
and it won't ask
if you're ready to go.
Son, your ride is leaving.

Read This Before You Die

It's
ok
to
float.
Heal up
and
push through.
But today
isn't for quitting.

Happen to your movement.
Birth the fight and spend it.

You will make new ways
without the people
that came with you.
They're busy on their own.

Someday is now,
somebody is you.

You are all you get.
For your entire life.

Always thinking you have more,
and then one day there won't be.

And you'll have lived a life
brimming with existence
or filled with excuses
for why you didn't.

What are you using this for?

The
  world
    doesn't
     owe
      you,
       or
        own
                you.

This
  stage
   was
    here
     before
                you.

Ok,
so you've had time
to figure out what hurts,
or that you can be.

There's.
More.
Ground to work.
Push it over.
Keep the mind moving through it.

You've come by it honestly.
Even if you don't land well.
Take a few breaths and grow.
Keep growing!
More today than yesterday.
As much as you feel you can stand.
Plant everything you can.
Even if you won't be around
to watch it grow.

Sleep it off,
or year it off.
Drop your shadow.
Start over.
Ball up,
and then stand up.
Keep the shadow
if it helps.
Show yourself.

Today
has
its
ways
of
demanding
your
presence.

Keep
digging.

There's
more
to
give.

Don't be afraid to bite
at what's keeping you there.
Repave it,
rework it.

This is it.

This is all you get.

This is your reminder.

Stop comparing your miracle
to everyone else's brick wall.
Today isn't for quitting.
Heal up and push through.
Happen to your movement.
Birth the fight.
You are alive.
What a thing to be alive,
to be anything at all.

While   the   piano   plays,
and   the   money   gets   counted,
and   the   pain   gets   folded
into   gratitude
gets   folded   into   your   day.

Everything.
Has.
A.
Turn.

You   earned this.
You   are a time machine.
The echo of your ancestors.
Always on the way,
and enough.

Read this before you die:

>This is it,
>right here.
>This is all we get.
>There's nothing else.
>You are it,
>in this moment.
>Pay attention.
>Be kind,
>to yourself.
>Follow your own map.
>Wake up and keep trying.

The Shapes We Make

Two lines
meet in the middle
'X' marks the spot.
Gather round.
Oh the shapes we make
when we intertwine.

```
Hold                    me                      down.
Don't           let             me              move.
With          your            finger            on.
These               frayed                      edges.
Jumping        through         the              hoops.
Tightening          what's                      loose.
On                  our                         shoes.
```

So tie me up.

     I'm rattling again-again.

Tongue tie me up.

     I'm babbling again my friend.

Don't tie me up.

     I'm out here traveling again.

          So tie me up,

          untie me,

          tie me up again.